The Promises Of Alcoholics Anonymous

and 12 Step Prayers

by Seth Goodman

ISBN: 9781797797069

DEDICATION

Dedicated to Bill W and Dr. Bob for starting a magnificent fellowship embodied by the program of Alcoholics Anonymous which was adopted from the Book of St. James and the Judeo Christianity tenants used in the Oxford movement and delivered the Bill by Ebby Thatcher who was a member, which were delivered to him by Rolland Hazard who was hence directed to the Oxford Group through shear desperation and the gift of information imparted upon him of the hopeless nature of the illness by Carl Jung.

The Promises
of Alcoholics Anonymous
by Seth Goodman

ISBN-13: 978-1717147127
ISBN-10: 1717147127
Seth Goodman

DEDICATION

This book is dedicated to all of those who've gone before us and so bravely paved the way for us to have it so easy. Sometimes we think we have it hard, or don't have any opportunities, but the opposite is the truth if we'd only follow the directions left for us we'd see clearly how easy it is and how wonderful life really can be.

CONTENTS

ACKNOWLEDGMENTS

I wish to acknowledge the amazing work of Bill W and Dr.Bob and all of the angels that made their journey both possible and probable. I would also like to acknowledge the amazing and unselfish work of Joe & Charlie, Chuck C., Joe Hawk, Jim P., and Sandy Beach for their extraordinary impact on the level of spiritual growth of Alcoholics Anonymous and many of it's members.

Seth Goodman

THE PROMISES OF
ALCOHOLICS ANONYMOUS

CHAPTER ONE
Step One Promises

The promises associated with completing all twelve steps:

1. The Story of How One Hundred Men and Women Have **Recovered from Alcoholism**. (Title Page)

2. WE, OF Alcoholics Anonymous, are more than one hundred men and woman who have recovered from a seemingly hopeless state of mind and body. To show other alcoholics **PRECISELY HOW WE HAVE RECOVERED** is the main purpose of this book. For them, we hope these pages will prove so convincing that no further authentication will be necessary. We think this account of our experiences will help everyone to better understand the alcoholic. Many do not comprehend that the alcoholic is a very sick person. And besides, we are sure that our way of living has its advantages for all. (Forward to the First Edition)

3. On the other hand - and strange as this may seem to those who do not understand- once a psychic change has occurred, the very same person who seemed doomed, who had so many problems he despaired of ever solving them, suddenly finds himself easily able to control his desire for alcohol, the only effort necessary being that required to follow a few simple rules. (Doctors Opinion (fifth page)

4. Nearly all have recovered. They have solved the drink problem. (17)

5. But, there exists among us a fellowship, a friendliness, and an understanding which is indescribably wonderful. (16)

6. The feeling of having shared in a common peril is one element in the powerful cement which binds us The tremendous fact for every one of us is that we have discovered a common solution. We have a way out on which we can absolutely agree, and upon which we can join in brotherly and harmonious action. This is the great news this book carries to those who suffer from alcoholism. (17)

7. **There is a solution.** (25)

8. But we saw that it really worked in others, and we had come to believe in the hopelessness and futility of life as we had been living it. (25)

9. We have found much of heaven and we have been rocketed into a fourth dimension of existence of which we had not even dreamed. (25)

10. The great fact is just this, and nothing less: That we have had deep and effective spiritual experiences which have revolutionized our whole attitude toward life, toward our fellows and toward God's universe. (25)

11. The central fact of our lives today is the absolute certainty that our Creator has entered into our hearts and lives in a way which is indeed miraculous. (25)

12. He has commenced to accomplish those things for us which we could never do by ourselves. (25)

13. We, in our turn, sought the same escape with all the desperation of drowning men. What seemed at first a flimsy reed, has proved to be the loving and powerful hand of God. A new life has been given us or, if you prefer, **"a design for living"** that **really works**. (28)

14. Further on, clear-cut directions are given showing how **we recovered**. (29)

15. Having had a spiritual awakening as the result of these steps, we tried to carry this message to alcoholics and to practice these principles in all our affairs. (60)

AT THE BEGINNING, YOU MAY NEED TO WORK REALLY HARD FOR JUST A LITTLE PROGRESS

The promises associated with Bill W.s Story:

1. I was soon to be catapulted into what I like to call the fourth dimension of existence. I was to know happiness, peace and usefulness, in a way of life that is incredibly more wonderful as time passes. (8)

2. God had done for him what he could not do for himself. (11)

3. Then he had, in effect, been raised from the dead, suddenly taken from the scrap heap to a level of life better than the best he had ever known. (11)

4. Thus I was convinced that God is concerned with us humans when we want him enough. At long last, I saw, I felt, I believed. Scales of pride and prejudice fell from my eyes. A new world came into view. (12)

5. My friend promised when those things were done, I would enter upon a new relationship with my Creator, that I would have the elements of a way of living which answered all my problems. (13)

6. These were revolutionary and drastic proposals but the moment I fully accepted them, the effect was electric. There was a sense of victory, followed by such a peace and serenity as I had never known. (14)

7. It is a design for living that works in rough going. (15)

8. We commenced to make many fast friends and a fellowship has grown up among us of which it is wonderful thing to feel a part. The joy of living we really have, even under pressure and difficulty. I have seen

hundreds of families set their feet in the path that really goes somewhere; have seen the most impossible domestic situations righted, feuds and bitterness of all sorts wiped out. I have seen men come out of asylums and resume a vital place in the lives of heir families and communities. Business and professional men have regained their standing. There is scarcely any form of trouble and misery which has not been overcome among us. (15)

9. There is, however, a vast amount of fun about it all. (15)

10. **Most of us feel we need look no further for Utopia**. We have it with us right here and now. Each day my friends simple talk in our kitchen multiplies itself in a widening circle of peace on earth and good will to men. (16)

SOON WE TAKE UP OUR BEDS AND WALK

The Promises Associated with Step One:

1. **Nearly all have recovered. They have solved the drink problem**. (17)

2. But, there exists among us a fellowship, a friendliness, and an understanding which is indescribably wonderful. (16)

3. The feeling of having shared in a common peril is one element in the powerful cement which binds us The

tremendous fact for every one of us is that we have discovered a common solution. We have a way out on which we can absolutely agree, and upon which we can join in brotherly and harmonious action. This is the great news this book carries to those who suffer from alcoholism. (17)

4. **There is a solution**. (25) *Thank God!*

5. But we saw that it really worked in others, and we had come to believe in the hopelessness and futility of life as we had been living it. (25)

6. We have found much of heaven and we have been rocketed into a fourth dimension of existence of which we had not even dreamed. (25)

7. The great fact is just this, and nothing less: That we have had deep and effective spiritual experiences which have revolutionized our whole attitude toward life, toward our fellows and toward God's universe. (25)

8. The central fact of our lives today is the absolute certainty that our Creator has entered into our hearts and lives in a way which is indeed **miraculous**. (25)

9. He has commenced to accomplish those things for us which we could never do by ourselves. (25)

10. We, in our turn, sought the same escape with all the desperation of drowning men. What seemed at first a flimsy reed, has proved to be the loving and powerful hand of God. A new life has been given us or, if you

prefer, "a design for living" that really works. (28)

11. Further on, clear-cut directions are given showing how we recovered. (29)

12. Yes, there is a substitute and it is vastly more than that. It is a fellowship in Alcoholics Anonymous. There you will find release from care, boredom and worry. Your imagination will be fired. Life will mean something at last. The most satisfactory years of your existence lie ahead. Thus we find the fellowship, and so will you. (152)You will be bound to them with new and wonderful ties, for you will escape disaster together and you will commence shoulder to shoulder your common journey. Then you will know what it means to give of yourself that others may survive and rediscover life. You will learn the full meaning of "Love thy neighbor as thyself." (152)

13. It may seem incredible that these men are to become happy, respected, and useful once more. How can they rise out of such misery, bad repute and hopelessness? The practical answer is that since these things have happened among us, they can happen with you. Should you wish them above all else, and be willing to make use of our experience, we are sure they will come. **The age of miracles is still with us**. Our own recovery proves that! (153)

14. Still you may say: "But I will not have the benefit of contact with you who wrote this book." We cannot be sure. God will determine that, so you must remember that your real reliance is always upon Him. **He will**

show you how to create the fellowship you crave.
(164)

15. Our book is meant to be suggestive only. We realize
we know only a little. **God will constantly disclose
more to you and to us**. Ask Him in your morning
meditation what you can do each day for the man who
is still sick. **The answers will come**, *if your own house
is in order*. But obviously you cannot transmit something
you haven't got. See to it that your relationship with Him
is right, and **great events will come to pass for you
and countless others**. This is the Great Fact for us.
(164)

16. We shall be with you in the Fellowship of the Spirit,
and you will surely meet some of us as you trudge
the Road of Happy Destiny. (164)

Step One offers each one of us a clear truth about our
condition. A major component of alcoholism is the
alcoholic mind and it's delusions. More About
Alcoholism repeats over and over, that the Alcoholic's
mind suffers from delusion, insanity and a strange
mental twist. Where it may be completely normal in
other matters, it becomes almost completely
incomprehensible in matter of alcohol.

This is a disease of perception, a mental illness of sorts
as so it is suggested, where "we cannot differentiate the
true from the false", or "see the beauty of the forrest
diverted by the ugliness of a few of the trees".

"What else could the complete and utter inability to think straight be called but plain insanity?"

Step One is: "We learned that we had to fully concede to **our innermost selves** that we were alcoholics. *This is the first step in recovery.*" Most of us can only do this after thoroughly going through all of step one admiringly with another human being well experienced with both drinking and recovery.

Not facing the truth about our conditions as illustrated by our drinking careers, we stand to begin to reason our way out of what could be an **ego deflating proposition.** Working these steps, although simple on paper, isn't easy for a real alcoholic in practice. It will take a definite understanding our our fate if we are to be convinced we need these steps in order to stay alive ourselves.

CHAPTER TWO
Step Two Promises

The promises associated with step two:

1. Well, thats exactly what this book is about. Its main object is to enable you to find a Power greater than yourself which will solve your problem. (45)

2. We found that as soon as we lay aside prejudice and expressed even a willingness to believe in a power greater than ourselves, we commenced to get results, even though it was impossible for any of us to fully define or comprehend that Power, which is God. (46)

3. Much to our relief, we discovered we did not need to consider another's conception of God. Our own conception, however inadequate, was sufficient to make the approach and to effect a contact with Him.(46)

4. As soon as we admitted the possible existence of a Creative Intelligence, a Spirit of the Universe underlying the totality of things, we began to be possessed of a new sense of power and direction, provided we took other simple steps. (46)

5. We found that God does not make too hard terms with those who seek Him. (46)

6. To us, the Realm of Spirit is broad, roomy, all inclusive; never exclusive or forbidding to those who earnestly seek. It is open, we believe, to all men. (46)

7.Afterward, we found ourselves accepting many things which then seemed entirely out of reach. (47)

8.As soon as a man can say that he does believe, or is willing to believe, we emphatically assure him that he is on his way. It has been repeatedly proven among us that upon this simple cornerstone a wonderfully effective spiritual structure can be built. (47)

9. Here are thousands of men and women, worldly indeed. They flatly declare that since they have come to believe in a Power greater than themselves, to take a certain attitude toward the Power, and to do certain simple things, there has been a revolutionary change in their way of living and thinking. (50)

10. In the face of collapse and despair, in the face of the total failure of their human resources, they found that a new power, peace, happiness, and sense of direction flowed into them. (50)

11. The outlines and the promise of the New Land had brought luster to tired eyes and fresh courage to flagging spirits. (53)

12. We finally saw that faith in some kind of God was a part of our make-up, just as much as the feeling we have for a friend. Sometimes we had to search fearlessly, but He was there. He was as much a fact as we were. (55)

13. We found the Great Reality deep down within us. In the last analysis it is only there that He may be found. It was so with us. (55)

14. If our testimony helps sweep away prejudice, enables you to think honestly, encourages you to search diligently within yourself, then if you wish you can join us on the Broad Highway. (55)

15. **With this attitude you cannot fail.** (55)

16. The consciousness of your belief is sure to come to you. (55)

17. Even so has God restored us all to our right minds. (57)

18. But He has come to all who have honestly sought Him. (57)

19. When we drew near to Him He disclosed Himself to us! (57)

20. Rarely have we seen a person fail who has thoroughly followed our path. (58)

Step Two isn't so much as saying you believe in a God or even a Higher Power, but more so, saying that **you are willing to acknowledge you aren't God** and that you willing to say you're not your own Higher Power.

This is a very important realization to come to, too many people get all caught up in the religious idea of a God, and lose sight of the fact this is an undoing process and Step Two is certainly at the very beginning of the undoing process.

There will be plenty of time to build your relationship with the God of your new understanding when you get there, don't mess things up again by trying to put the cart before the horse, it just doesn't work that way. Hopefully, you have a good mentor in AA to show you this, but however, unfortunately, there are plenty of people who have tie yet and still don't understand this simple concept.

CHAPTER THREE
Step Three Promises

The promises associated with step three:

1. a) That we were alcoholic and could not manage our own lives. and, b) That probably no human power could have relieved our alcoholism.c) That God could and would if he were sought. (60)

2. Above everything, we alcoholics must be rid of this selfishness. We must, or it kills us! God makes that possible. (62)

3. Most good ideas are simple, and this concept was the keystone of the new and triumphant arch through which we passed to freedom. (62)

4. When we sincerely took such a position, all sort of remarkable things followed. (63)

5. We had a new Employer. (63)

6. Being all powerful, He provided what we needed, if we kept close to Him and performed His work well. (63)

7. Established on such a footing we became less and less interested in ourselves, our little plans and designs. (63)

8. More and more we became interested in seeing what we could contribute to life. (63)

9. As we felt new power flow in, as we enjoyed peace of mind, as we discovered we could face life successfully, as we became conscious of His presence, we began to lose our fear of today, tomorrow or the hereafter. (63)

10. **We were reborn.** (63)

11. This was only the beginning, though if honestly and humbly made, an effect, sometimes a very great one, was felt at once. (63)

Step Three is a place where we let go of our will and test our trust in the process placed at our feet along with a sponsor and the set of direction laid out for us in the Big Book of Alcoholics Anonymous.

The excellent news about this, is that if any of these variables don't work for you immediately, you can try them again and again, until they do. The program will always be the same, only your willingness and degree of skill through practice will vary, and it will continuously get better the more you work them into your life.

In effect, it's always **little by slowly,** as we make our progress, you'll see it goes two steps forward one step back. But staying the course will always yield great results and the joy of living will come for all who embark upon this journey.

No one does this thing perfectly, many will try to hide their shortcomings rather than lose face because of pride. Don't think you're any less of one of God's perfect children than anyone else, or deserve sobriety any less, because you certainly do!

CHAPTER FOUR
Step Four Promises

The promises associated with step four:

1. When the spiritual malady is overcome, **we start to straighten out mentally and physically**. (64)

2. We cannot be helpful to all people but at least God will show us how to take a kindly and tolerant view of each and every one. (67)

3. Just to the extent that we do what we think He would have of us and humbly rely on Him, **does He enable us to match calamity with serenity**. (68)

4. We ask him to remove our fear and direct our attention to what he would have us be. At once, **we commence to outgrow fear**. (68)

5. In meditation, we ask God what we should do about each specific matter. **The right answer will come**, if we want it. (69)

6. If we are sorry for what we have done, and have the honest desire to let God take us to better things, we believe **we will be forgiven** and will have learned our lesson. (70)

7. We have begun to comprehend their futility and their fatality. (70)

8. We have commenced to see their terrible destructiveness. (70)

9. **We have begun to learn tolerance, patience and good will toward all men**, even our enemies, for we look on the them as sick people. (70)

10. We hope you are convinced now that **God can remove whatever self-will has blocked you** off from Him. (70)

Step Four is a major cleansing of our character. I've always said that "Our Character Defects cause our Short Comings". It's as if my arm is too weak to make the basket hoop, an my shots continuously come up short. Through the steps, we strengthen our arm (God's Power) and begin making these shots and through which become a useful member of the team.

Then, what would happen??

People will start to want me around, they'll give me responsibilities, they'll pay me better, and I'll finally feel significant, again, maybe for the very first time in my life.

Whenever I get a resentment, have a fear, or have a looming sense of guilt due to a harm I've caused another person; I restrict my inherent ability because I've become in discord with my Creator just a little bit more. This discord, then forces me to be that much more "Self-Reliant" because I am losing the Power originally given to me by God.

When I lose power, my default is to lie, cheat and steal in order to feel that my needs are getting met. One of my greatest needs are to feel significant, to feel worthy, to feel accepted. So feeling I've lost power, I must gain power, thus, I work to overpower my brothers and cheat them when I can. This back fires and eventually gain power, thus, I work to overpower my brothers and cheat them when I can. This back fires and eventually I'm alone, lonely and didn't get anything I thought I needed.

CHAPTER FIVE
Step Five Promises

The promises associated with step five:

1. Once we have taken this step, withholding nothing, we are delighted. (75)

2. We can look the world in the eye. (75)

3. We can be alone at perfect peace and ease. (75)

4. Our fears fall from us. (75)

5. We begin to feel the nearness of our Creator. (75)

6. We may have had certain spiritual beliefs, but now we begin to have a spiritual experience. (75)

7. The feeling that the drink problem has disappeared will often come strongly. (75)

8. We feel we are on the Broad Highway, walking hand in hand with the Spirit of the Universe. (75)

9. Carefully reading the first five proposals we ask if we have omitted anything, for we are building an arch through which we shall walk a free man at last. (75)

Wow! Step Five really delivers a lot of what we didn't know it had to give us. The freedom, and to be a part of AA at last. To know that we were as bad or as guilty as we thought, that our resentments were not even true as soon as we spoke them out loud we almost felt foolish.

And that everyone has fears and we all pretty much have the same ones, and most of them don't ever come true, they're mostly illusions made up in my own mind, and when i don't value them, they fo away.

Remember that Step Five includes sitting alone with God for One (full) Hour, in Prayer and meditation, quiet. Looking at if there is anything you left out, if you've slipped on the sand you put into the mortar as we are building an archway through which we are going to pass into freedom.

If there is anything that we've left out, we are sure to write it down and call our step sponsor immediately following the hour, to let them know what it is, talk about it, go through it just as we've gone through everything else.

Chances are that this "thing" isn't as bad as we thought it was. If we've chosen the right step sponsor, if it is a difficult one, they are sure to have the patience, tolerance and understanding, to go through it with you as best they can. helping as much as possible with it.

"We found a solitary self-self-appraisal insufficient".

We cannot skip this step, if we have written a fourth step and delay going through the fifth step, to ghosts of our past are out of their bag and will haunt us with a unrelenting vengeance. Remember we said we were wiling to go to any length for history over alcoholism.

CHAPTER SIX
Step Six Prayers

The promises associated with step six:

1. We have emphasized willingness as being indispensable. (76)

2. Are we now ready to let God remove from us all things which are objectionable? (76)

3. Can He take them all every one?

4. If we cling to something we will not let go, we ask God to help us be willing. (76)

The mercy is in the **humility** of this step. In step Six we're preparing to let God in and work a miracle with our brokenness. We've been making a wreck of things for a long time, things continue to get worse and our drinking was out of control, we're dying and hurting others in the process, others whom we loved.

Of course I'm willing, I have to be. I just took a good hard look at the "stock in trade", of my life and I pretty much have a garage dump in the store room where I'm supposed to be trying to run business. No wonder it's not working out. Looking at a warehouse of defective crap called my mind's own creations, I'm literally sickened by it to the point where everything in it is objectionable.

Of course, we are delusional, outright mental defectives and for the most part, cannot differentiate the true from the false. So, we find some insane reason why something shouldn't go… this is one point where, the insane idea wins out and we hold onto some of the worst items in stock. Eventually thought they prove to be what they are and we have to let them go, often after paying a hefty price for holding onto them though.

CHAPTER SEVEN
Step Seven Promises

The promises associated with step seven:

1. When **we're ready**... (76)

2. My Creator **I am now willing**... (76)

3. I pray the you remove from me every single defect of character... (76)

4. **my usefulness** to You and my fellows. (76)

5. Grant me Strength to do Your bidding. (76)

Step seven is my understanding that I don't have the strength to stop drinking on my own, to make choices or correct character defects. If anything, ego and pride has proven stronger than self in this case. I must enlist a Power greater then myself to conquer my foe's in order to arise victorious.

Again, **my willingness to change and** to **not** be that person who walked in here, to surrender my ideas, plans and schemes, is the single factor that will catapult me over this hurdle.

The Sixth and Seventh Step are the **Pivotal** steps of the entire program. They are the moment of change. The **willingness** to do so, knowing full well we completely lack any power to do so, we surrender all rights to withhold any defect of character so that **God** can build us into the human form of a gift of grace much greater than our fearful and guilty frozen minds could've ever fathomed from these states.

CHAPTER EIGHT
Step Eight Promises

The promise associated with step eight:

1. If that degree of humility could **enable us to find the grace by which such a deadly obsession could be banished,** then there must be hope of the same result respecting any other problem we could possibly have.(12&12 76)

2. We attempt to sweep away the debris which has accumulated out of our effort to live on self-will and run the show ourselves. (76)

3. *We remember that we agreed we would go to any length for victory over alcohol.* (76)

Step eight is gearing us up to become the grown-ups that we set out to do at the beginning. This is home plate and without completing this process all of our work up until this would have for nothing. The growth, the experiences, the people we found who actually care and authentically helped us, all gone.

This is a matter of life and death,
if we don't recover,
we will drink - and to drink is to die.

There are only two options, I either continue to expand my spiritual life and that means continue to thoroughly practice all of the steps in every instance, or spiritual death, which is where I came from.

CHAPTER NINE
Step Nine Promises

The promises associated with step nine:

1. If our manner is calm, frank, and open, we will be gratified with the result. (78)

2. In nine cases out of ten the unexpected happens. Sometimes the man we are calling upon admits his own faults, so feuds of years' standing melt away in an hour. (78)

3. Rarely do we fail to make satisfactory progress. (78)

4. If we are painstaking about this phase of our development, we will be amazed before we are half way through. (83)

5. We are going to know a new freedom and a new happiness. (83)

6. We will not regret the past nor wish to shut the door on it. (83)

7. We will comprehend the word serenity and we will know peace. (83)

8. No matter how far down the scale we have gone, we will see how our experience can benefit others. (84)

9. That feeling of uselessness and self-pity will disappear. (84)

10. We will lose interest in selfish things and gain interest in our fellows.(84)

11. Self-seeking will slip away.(84)

12. Our whole attitude and outlook upon life will change. (84)

13. Fear of people and of economic insecurity will leave us. (84)

14. We will intuitively know how to handle situations which used to baffle us. (84)

15. We will suddenly realize that **God is doing for us** what we could not do for ourselves. (84)

16. Are these extravagant promises? We think not. They are being fulfilled among us, sometimes quickly, sometimes slowly. *They will always materialize if we work for them.* (84)

After doing all of our amends we see may of these materialize in all areas of our lives. We will be amazed by the promises appearing in our lives before we are halfway through the amends process, the Big Book also promises this.

We will definitely have a more hands on understanding that our FEARS are False Emotions Appearing Real... because when we walk with God with the right purpose and intention, humbly as He directs us, He is there with us and makes the situation work, so that we can once again draw closer to Him.

When drinking, we avoided handling situations where conflict would arise and when we did have to face it, we usually didn't handle it with humility, dignity or grace. Practicing making amends on some of the wrong doing of our past will help us to quickly make amends when we are wrong in our daily lives through practicing our step ten.

CHAPTER TEN
Step Ten Promises

The promises associated with step ten:

1. And we have ceased fighting anything or anyone even alcohol. (84)

2. For by this time sanity will have returned. (84)

3. We will seldom be interested in liquor.

4. If tempted, we recoil from it as from a hot flame. (84)

5. We react sanely and normally, and we will find that this has happened automatically. (85)

6. We will see that our new attitude toward liquor has been given us without any thought or effort on our part. It just comes! That is the miracle of it. (85)

7. We are not fighting it, neither are we avoiding temptation. (85)

8. We feel as though we had been placed in a position of neutrality, safe and protected. (85)

9. We have not even sworn off. Instead, the problem has been removed. It does not exist for us. (85)

10. We are neither cocky nor are we afraid. That is our experience. That is how we react so long as we keep in fit spiritual condition. (85)

11. If we have carefully followed directions, we have begun to sense the flow of His Spirit into us. (85)

12. To some extent we have become God-conscious. (85)

13. We have begun to develop this vital six sense. (85)

In Step Ten we practice these principles all through out our day. When Anger, Self-Pity, Worry or Excitement show up, **we pause** and take the appropriate actions as indicated in the previous steps, Do I owe an apology, do I need to right a wrong? These steps do not come naturally at first, but after practicing them, the become second nature.

The whole part of mindfulness, this philosophy helps us to see things as they really are, not with all of the disturbance and confusion that selfish motivate had always caused us. In the beginning this goes very slow and the temptation is to hurry through things and not experience the awareness of your self in different situations.

Then we are practicing forgiveness, undoubtedly situation will arise throughout your day that incite antipathy, anger and resentment. Maybe spark and old wound you previously assumed had healed and was gone. This is a great time to re-practice the steps and procedures that would re-connect you with God.

Throughout all of this, the one thing that is constant is your relationship with God. This is the Source for the Power we lack. We go back and forth day in and day out, ebbing and flowing close to and away from, this Source. When we're close, life seems to get easier, when we get distant, it seems to get more difficult.

The drama of life really has us in it's grips. We need to find a new balance in which we can be in this world, but not of this world.

We cannot depend on worldly things, events, people, happenings, to make us whole, serene and peaceful, this will never happen for us. that sense of being has to come from the inside out. We can no longer buy the lie that we could be happy if we could only wrest satisfaction out of life.

CHAPTER ELEVEN
Step Eleven Promises

The promises associated with step eleven:

1. Step Eleven suggests prayer and meditation. ....It
   works, if we have the proper attitude and work at it.
   (86)

2. Under these conditions we can employ our mental
faculties with assurance, for after all God gave us
brains to use. (86)

3. Our thought-life will be placed on a much higher
plane when our thinking is cleared of wrong
motives. (86)

4. In thinking about our day we may face indecision. We may not be able to determine which course to take. Here we ask God for inspiration, an intuitive thought or a decision. We relax and take it easy. We don't struggle. We are often surprised how the right answers come after we have tried this for a while. (86)

5. What used to be the hunch or the occasional inspiration gradually becomes a working part of the mind. (87)

6. Nevertheless, we find that our thinking will, as time passes, be more and more on the plane of inspiration. We come to rely upon it. (87)

7. We are then in much less danger of excitement, fear, anger, worry, self-pity, or foolish decisions. (88)

8. We become much more efficient. (88)

9. We do not tire so easily, for we are not burning up energy foolishly as we did when we were trying to arrange life to suit ourselves. (88)

10. It works, it really does. (88)

Step eleven is Nightly Inventory, Prayer and Meditation. This is a process by where we really start to connect to the Power of God that we, as humans, and even more so as alcoholics, lack.

The is the missing element that caused such drama and chaos in our lives. It takes just a few minutes to do a nightly review of our day, surprisingly 80% of our members don't do it.

Sadly, it's one of the most important works to be continued in our daily practice of these steps.

How am I to know what exactly is right or wrong in my affairs throughout my day if I don't inventory them? How will I know what to ask God to remove if I haven't seen where my defects are objectionable, will I even think I've done anything wrong?

Probably not. The truth is that sometimes after we've gone through the step process, we rest on our achievements, thinking "look what I've accomplished, I deserve a rest".

When in all honesty, this entire program and all of the results witnessed from it, are all a part of God's Grace and Love for you. They're gifts.

I have to remember this so that all of the noise this world generates doesn't attract me into it, the drama, helping me to forget who and what I am. A Real (sick) Alcoholic.

CHAPTER TWELVE
Step Twelve Promises

The promises associated with step twelve:

1. PRACTICAL EXPERIENCE shows that nothing will
so much insure immunity from drinking as
intensive work with other alcoholics. It works when other
activities fail. (89)

2. **Life will take on new meaning**. (89)

3. To watch people recover, to see them help others, to
watch loneliness vanish, to see a fellowship grow up
about you, to have a host of friends this is **an
experience you must not miss**. We know you will not
want to miss it. Frequent contact with newcomers and
with each other is **the bright spot of our lives**. (89)

4. Both you and the new man must walk day by day in the path of spiritual progress. If you persist, **remarkable things will happen**. (100)

5. When we look back, we realize that the things which came to us when we put ourselves in God's hands were **better than anything we could have planned**. (100)

6. Follow the dictates of a Higher Power and **you will presently live in a new and wonderful world**, no matter what your present circumstances! (100)

7. Assuming we are spiritually fit, **we can do all sorts of things** alcoholics are not supposed to do. (100)

8. Your job now is to be at the place where you may be of maximum helpfulness to others, so never hesitate to go anywhere if you can be helpful. You should not hesitate to visit the most sordid spot on earth on such an errand. Keep on the firing line of life with these motives and **God will keep you unharmed**. (102)

9. **The power of God goes deep!** (102)

10. We have stopped fighting anybody and anything. We have to! (103)

Step Twelve is two parts of a whole. The first part is continuing to carry this message as well as making it possible that others carry this message, both of which everyone should be doing. Some folks think they're designed to only do service work and not sponsorship, this is a grave mistake and will only shortchange them in they spiritual growth. Sponsorship as well as service work, making twelve step work possible, is imperative, essential and vital to the program of each individual.

The second part of step Twelve are displayed by my actions, attitudes and behaviors, all through the day.

What message am I sending to the world, the universe, my Creator, about sobriety, the sober life and the program of Alcoholics Anonymous?

Am I still behaving poorly, refusing to change old behaviors? These all reflect poorly on a program that has saved my life.

Eventually the distance we place between God and ourself, through the thoughts, words and deeds we exhibit will culminate into our inability to handle life on life's terms, where a drink will become the ultimate sacrifice to a new and wonderful life we've been granted by the grace of a wonderful and powerful all-loving Creator.

BONUS CHAPTER

Promises associated with the "Lost Chapters."

1. There is every evidence that women regain their health as readily as men if they try our suggestions (104)

2. We want to leave you with the feeling that no situation is too difficult and no unhappiness to great to be overcome. (104)

3. Yet often such men had spectacular and powerful recoveries. (113)

4. The power of God goes deep. (114)

5. But sometimes you must start life anew. We know women who have done it. If such women adopt a spiritual way of life their road will be smoother. (114)

6. When you have carefully explained to such people that he is a sick person, you will have created a new atmosphere. Barriers which have sprung up between you and your friends will disappear with the growth of sympathetic understanding. You will no longer be self-conscious or feel that you must apologize as though your husband were a weak character. He may be anything but that. Your new courage, good nature and lack of self-consciousness will do wonders for you socially. (115)

7. We have elsewhere remarked how much better life is when lived on a spiritual plane. If God can solve the age-old riddle of alcoholism, He can solve your problems too. (116)

8. Now we try to put spiritual principles to work in our lives. When we do that, we find it solves our problems too; the ensuing lack of fear, worry and hurt feelings is a wonderful thing. (116)

9. If you and your husband find a solution for the pressing problem of drink you are, of course, going to be very happy. (117)

10. The faith and sincerity of you and your husband will be put to the test. These work-outs should be regarded as part of your education, for thus you will be learning to live. You will make mistakes, but if you are in earnest

they will not drag you down. Instead you will capitalize them. A better way of life will emerge when they are overcome. (117)

11. When resentful thoughts come, try to pause and count your blessings. After all, your family is reunited, alcohol is no longer a problem and you and your husband are working together toward an undreamed of future. (119)

12. Both of you will awaken to a new sense of responsibility for others. (119)

13. You will lose the old life to find one much better. (120)

14. Showing others who suffer how we were given help is the very thing which makes life seem so worth while to us now. Cling to the thought that in, Gods hands, the dark past is the greatest possession you have - they key to life and happiness for others. With it you can avert death and misery for them. (124)

15. Let them remember that his drinking wrought all kinds of damage that may take long to repair. If they sense these things, they will not take so seriously his periods of crankiness, depression, or apathy, which will disappear when there is tolerance, love, and spiritual understanding. (127)

16. Giving, rather than getting, will become the guiding principle. (128)

17. Joy at our release from a lifetime of frustration knew no bounds. (128)

18. If the family cooperated, dad will soon see that he is suffering from a distortion of values. He will perceive that his spiritual growth is lopsided, that for an average man like himself, a spiritual life which does not include his family obligations may not be so perfect after all. If the family will appreciate that dads current behavior is but a phase of his development, all will be well. In the midst of an understanding and sympathetic family, these vagaries of dads spiritual infancy will quickly disappear. (129)

19. Those of us who have spent much time in the world of spiritual make-believe have eventually seen the childishness of it. This dream world has been replaced by a great sense of purpose, accompanied by a growing consciousness of the power of God in our lives. We have come to believe He would like us to keep our heads in the clouds with Him, but that our feet ought to be firmly planted on earth. That is where our fellow travelers are, and that is where our work must be done. These are the realities for us. We have found nothing incompatible between a powerful spiritual experience and a life of sane and happy usefulness. (130)

20. We are sure God wants us to be happy, joyous, and free.

21. We are convinced that a spiritual mode of living is most powerful restorative. We, who have recovered

from serious drinking, are miracles of mental health. But we have seen remarkable transformations in our bodies. Hardly one of our crowd now shows any mark of dissipation. (133)

22. In time they will see that he is a new man and in their own way they will let him know it. When this happens, they can be invited to join in morning meditation and then they can take part in the daily discussion without rancor or bias. From that point on, progress will be rapid. Marvelous results often follow such a reunion. (134)

*Parenthesis (-) indicate the page number where the promise is found in the Big Book of Alcoholics Anonymous.

The Twelve Step Prayers from the Big Book of Alcoholics Anonymous

The Set-Aside Prayer:

"Dear God, please help me to set aside, everything I think I know about the Twelve Steps, the Fellowship, my illness, and You God, so that I may have an open mind and a new experience with all these things. Please help me to see the truth. AMEN."
(This prayer comes from the Chapter to the Agnostic, primarily pages 47 and 48).

First Step Prayer

Dear Lord, Help me to see and admit that I am powerless over my alcoholism. Help me to understand how my alcoholism has led to unmanageability in my life. Help me this day to understand the true meaning of powerlessness. Remove from me all denial of my alcoholism. (This prayer is developed from the chapter, More About Alcoholism)

A Second Step Prayer

Heavenly Father, I am having trouble with my personal relationships. I can't control my emotional nature. I am prey to misery and depression. I can't seem to make a living. I feel useless. I am full of fear. I am unhappy. I can't seem to be of real help to others. I know in my heart that only you can restore me to sanity if I am just willing to stop doubting your power. I humbly ask that you help me to understand that, it is more powerful to believe than not to believe, and that You are either everything or You can be nothing at all. (p. 52:2, 52:3, 53:1, 53:2)

3rd Step Prayer:

"God, I offer myself to thee - to build with me and do with me as Thou wilt. Relieve me of the bondage of self, that I may better do Thy will. Take away my difficulties, that victory over them may bear witness to those I would help of Thy Power, Thy Love and Thy Way of life. May I do Thy will always!" (63:2 original manuscript)

A Pre-Inventory Prayer:

"God, please help me to honestly take stock. Help me to search out the flaws in my make-up which caused my failure. Help me to see where resentment has plagued me and resulted in spiritual malady, but more importantly help me to understand my part in these resentments. Help me to resolutely look for my own mistakes and to understand where I had been selfish, dishonest, self-seeking and frightened. Please help me to be searching and fearless in my endeavor to write my inventory." (p. 64:2, 64:3, 67:2)

A 4th Step Resentment Prayer:

"God, Please help me to be free of anger and to see that the world and its people have dominated me. Show me that the wrong-doing of others, fancied or real, has the power to actually kill me. Help me to master my resentments by understanding that the people who wrong me were perhaps spiritually sick. Please help me show those I resent the same Tolerance, Pity and Patience that I would cheerfully grant a sick friend.** Help me to see that this is a sick man. Father, please show me how I can be helpful to him and save me from being angry. Lord, help me to avoid retaliation or argument. I know I can't be helpful to all people, but at least show me how to take a kindly and tolerant view of each and every one. Thy will be done."(66:2, 66:3, 66:4, 67:0, 67:1)

**Dear God, I have a resentment towards a person that I want to be free of. So, I am asking you to give this person everything I want for myself. Help me to feel compassionate understanding and love for this person. I pray that they will receive everything they need. Thank you God for your help and strength with this resentment. (BB, Freedom from Bondage: 552)

These instructions are for the above prayer (Big Book, Freedom from Bondage, p. 552):

'If you have a resentment you want to be free of, if you will pray for the person or the thing that you resent, you will be free. If you will ask in prayer for everything you want for yourself to be given to them, you will be free...Even when you don't really want it for them, and your prayers are only words and you don't mean it, go ahead and do it anyway. Do it every day for two weeks and you will find you have come to mean it and to want it for them, and you will realize that where you used to feel bitterness and resentment and hatred, you now feel compassionate understanding and love".You can, also, include the Freedom from Bondage Prayer in the 4th Step Resentment Prayer.

An Example of a Fear Prayer:

"God, thank you for helping me be honest enough to see this truth about myself and now that you have shown me the truth about my fears, please remove these fears from me. Lord, please help me outgrow my fears and direct my attention to what you would have me be. Father, demonstrate through me and help me become that which you would have me be. Help me do thy will always, Amen."(68:3)

An Example of a Pre-Sex Inventory Prayer:

"God, please help me to be free of fear as I attempt to shine the spotlight of truth across my past sex relations. Lord, please show me where my behavior has harmed others and help me to see the truth these relationships hold for me. Help me see where I have been at fault and what I should have done differently." (From the thoughts on pg. 69)

"God, help me review my own conduct over the years past. Show me where I have been selfish, dishonest, or inconsiderate. Show me whom I have hurt and where I have unjustifiably aroused jealousy, suspicion or bitterness. Help me to see where I was at fault and what I should have done instead. Help me to be fearless and searching in my endeavor to write my sexual inventory." (69:1)

A Sex Ideals Prayer

"Father, please help me mold my sex ideals and help me to live up to them. Help me be willing to grow toward my ideals and help me be willing to make amends where I have done harm. Lord, please show me what to do in each specific matter, and be the final judge in each situation. Help me avoid hysterical thinking or advice." (69:2, 69:3)

"Father, please Grace me with guidance in each questionable situation, sanity, and strength to do the right thing. If sex becomes very troublesome, quiet my imperious urge, help me not to yield and keep me from heartache as I throw myself the harder into helping others. Help me think of their needs and help me work for them. Amen." (69:2, 69:3, 70:2)

A Pre-Fifth Step Prayer

God, please help me to complete my housecleaning by admitting to another human being the exact nature of my wrongs. Please remove any fears I have about this step and show me how completion of it will remove my egotism and fear. Help me to see how this step builds my character through humility, fearlessness and honesty. Direct me to the right person who will keep my confidence and fully understand and approve what I am driving at. Then help me to pocket my pride and go to it, illuminating every twist of character, every dark cranny of the past so I may complete this step and begin to feel near to you." (72:1, 72:2, 73:0, 74:2, 75:2)

A Fifth Step Prayer

Higher Power, Thank you for helping me complete my housecleaning. I can now look the world in the eye. I can be alone at perfect peace and ease. My fears have fallen from me. I have begun to feel your nearness. I have begun to have a spiritual experience. I feel I am on the Broad Highway, walking hand in hand with the Spirit of the Universe. (75:2)

A Quiet Hour Prayer:

"God, Thank You for giving me the strength, faith and courage I needed to get through my 5th Step. I thank you from the bottom of my heart for helping me to know you better, by showing me what has been blocking me from you. Father, please show me if I have omitted anything and help me to honestly see if my stones are properly in place or if I have skimped in any area of this work."(75:3)

A 6th Step Prayer:

"God, Thank you for removing my fear and for showing me the truth about myself. Father, I need your help to become willing to let go of the things in me which continue to block me off from you. Please grant me your Grace Lord and make me willing to have these objectionable characteristics, defects and shortcomings removed." (76:1)

A Sixth Step Prayer

Dear God, I am ready for Your help in removing from me the defects of character which I now realize are an obstacle to my recovery. Help me to continue being honest with myself & guide me toward spiritual & mental health. (76:1)

A Seventh Step Prayer

"My Creator, I am now willing that you should have all of me, good & bad. I pray that you now remove from me every single defect of character which stands in the way of my usefulness to you & my fellows. Grant me strength, as I go out from here to do Your bidding." (76:2)

A Pre-Eighth Step Prayer

"God, Please remove my Fears and show me your truth. Show me all the harms I have caused with my behavior and help me be willing to make amends to one and all. Help me to be willing to go to any lengths for victory over alcohol."(76:3)

A 9th Step Prayer:

"God, with regard to this amend, give me the strength, courage and direction to do the right thing, no matter what the personal consequences may be. Help me not to shrink from anything. Help me not to delay if it can be avoided. Help me to be sensible, tactful, considerate and humble without being servile or scraping."(79:1, 83:3)

A 9th Step Prayer for the Spouse::

"God, please show me how to make amends to my Spouse. Father , Help me to keep my Spouse's happiness Uppermost in my mind as I try, with your Grace, to make this relationship right. Amen" (82:1)

A 9Th Step Prayer for the Family:

"God, please show me how to find the way of Patience, Tolerance, Kindness and Love in my heart, my Mind and my Soul. Lord, show me how to demonstrate these principles to my family and all those about me. Amen." (83:1)

A 10th Step Prayer for Growth and Effectiveness:

"God, please help me Watch for Selfishness, Dishonesty, Resentment and Fear. When these crop up in me, help me to immediately ask you to remove them from me and help me discuss these feelings with someone. Father, help me to quickly make amends if I have harmed anyone and help me to resolutely turn my thoughts to someone I can Help. Help me to be Loving and Tolerant of everyone today. Amen"(84:2)

Tenth Step Prayer

My Higher Power, My daily prayer is to best serve you, I pray I may continue to grow in understanding & effectiveness; Help me to watch for selfishness, dishonesty, resentment and fear; Help me to be willing to have You remove them at once; I must be willing to discuss them with someone immediately; I will make amends quickly if I have harmed anyone; And then I will turn my thoughts toward helping someone else; Please help me to remember to practice love and tolerance of others. (84:2)

Tenth Step Amends Prayers

"God, please forgive me for my failings today. I know that because of my failings, I was not able to be as effective as I could have been for you. Please forgive me and help me live thy will better today. I ask you now to show me how to correct the errors I have just outlined. Guide me and direct me. Please remove my arrogance and my fear. Show me how to make my relationships right and grant me the humility and strength to do thy will."(86:1)

The 11th Step Prayers:

A Prayer on Awakening

"God please direct my thinking and keep my thoughts divorced from self – pity, dishonest or self-seeking motives. Please keep my thought life clear from wrong motives and help me employ my mental faculties, that my thought-life might be placed on a higher plane, the plane of inspiration." (86:2)

A Morning Prayer:
"God, should I find myself agitated, doubtful or indecisive today, please give me inspiration, help me to have an intuitive thought or a decision about this problem I face. Help me not to struggle, instead, help me to relax and take it easy. Help me know what I should do and keep me mindful, that you are running the show. Free me from my bondage of self. Thy will be done always." (86:3)

A Morning Prayer:
"God, please show me all through this day, what my next step is to be and please grace me with whatever I need to take care of the problems in my life today. I ask especially that you free me from the bondage of self-will."(87:1)

An 11th Step Nightly Review Prayer:
"God, help me to constructively review my day. Where was I resentful, selfish, dishonest or afraid? Do I owe an apology? Have I kept something to myself which should be discussed with another person at once? Was I kind and loving toward all? What could I have done better? Was I thinking of myself most of the time? Or, was I thinking of what I could do for others, of what I could pack into the stream of life? Please forgive me for my harms and wrongs today and let me know corrective measures I should be take." (86:2)

Prayer of Saint Francis

Lord make me an instrument of your peace Where there

is hatred let me sow love

Where there is injury, pardon

Where there is doubt, faith

Where there is despair, hope

Where there is darkness, light

And where there is sadness, joy

O divine master grant that I may

not so much seek to be consoled as to console to be

understood as to understand

To be loved as to love

For it is in giving that we receive

it is in pardoning that we are pardoned And it's in dying

that we are born to eternal life Amen

Twelfth Step Prayer

Dear God, Having had a spiritual experience, I *must* now remember that "faith without works is dead." And PRACTICAL EXPERIENCE shows that nothing will so much insure immunity from drinking as intensive work with other alcoholics. So, God, please help me to carry this message to other alcoholics! Provide me with the guidance and wisdom to talk with another alcoholic because I can help when no one else can. Help me secure his confidence and remember he is ill. (89:1)

The Big Book

"MUSTS" (or, Have To Do's)

"Our book is meant to be suggestive only. We realize we know only a little. God will constantly disclose more to you and to us . Ask Him in your morning meditation what you can do each day for the man who is still sick.

The answers will come, if your own house is in order. But obviously you cannot transmit something you haven't got. See to it that your relationship with Him is right, and great events will come to pass for you and countless others. This is the Great Fact for us." Big Book, page 164

While the program is considered a suggested method for dealing with the illness of Alcoholism, there are places within the Big Book where the authors used the word '**MUST**.' The following is a list of the 40 Musts from the Big Book.

1. He suddenly realized that in order to save himself he <u>must</u> carry his message to another alcoholic.
(Forward to the 2nd Edition)

2. In this statement he confirms what we who have suffered alcoholic torture must believe--t*hat the body of the alcoholic is quite as abnormal as his mind.* (The Doctor's Opinion)

3. The message which can interest and hold these alcoholic people must have depth and weight. (The Doctor's Opinion)

4. In nearly all cases, their ideals must be grounded in a power greater than themselves, if they are to recreate their lives. (The Doctor's Opinion)

5. Simple, but not easy; a price had to be paid. It meant destruction of self-centeredness. I must turn in all things to the Father of Light who presides over us all. (Bill's Story)

6. If we are planning to stop drinking, there must be no reservation of any kind, nor any lurking notion that someday we will be immune to alcohol. (33)

7. Once more: The alcoholic at certain times has no effective mental defense against the first drink. Except in a few cases, neither he nor any other human being can provide such a defense. His defense must come from a Higher Power. (43)

8. But after a while we had to face the fact that we must find a spiritual basis of life --or else. (44)

9. They arise out of ourselves, and the alcoholic is an extreme example of self-will run riot, though he usually

doesn't think so. Above everything, we alcoholics must be rid of this selfishness. We <u>must</u>, or it kills us! God makes that possible. (62)

10. We began to see that the world and its people really dominated us. In that state, the wrong-doing of others, fancied or real, had power to actually kill. How could we escape? We saw that these resentments <u>must</u> be mastered, but how? We could not wish them away any more than alcohol. (66)

11. Whatever our ideal turns out to be, we <u>must</u> be willing to grow toward it. We must be willing to make amends where we have done harm, provided that we do not bring about still more harm in so doing. In other words, we treat sex as we would any other problem. in meditation, we ask God what we should do about each specific matter. The right answer will come, if we want it. (69)

12. We must be entirely honest with somebody if we expect to live long or happily in this world. Rightly and naturally, we think well before we choose the person or persons with whom to take this intimate and confidential step. Those of us belonging to a religious denomination which requires confession <u>must</u>, and of course, will want to go to the properly appointed authority whose duty it is to receive it. (73)

13. The rule is we <u>must</u> be hard on ourself, but always considerate of others. (74)

14. We say this because we are very anxious that we talk to the right person. It is important that he be able to keep a confidence; that he fully understand and approve what we are driving at; that he will not try to change our plan. But we <u>must</u> not use this as a mere excuse to postpone. (74)

15. Our drinking has made us slow to pay. We <u>must</u> lose our fear of creditors no matter how far we have to go, for we are liable to drink if we are afraid to face them. (78)

16. Although these reparations take innumerable forms, there are some general principles which we find guiding. Reminding ourselves that we have decided to go to any lengths to find a spiritual experience, we ask that we be given strength and direction to do the right thing, no matter what the personal consequences may be. We may lose our position or reputation or face jail, but we are willing. We have to be. We <u>must</u> not shrink at anything. (79)

17. Before taking drastic action which might implicate other people we secure their consent. If we have obtained permission, have consulted with others, asked God to help and the drastic step is indicated we <u>must</u> not shrink. (80)

18. Sometimes we hear an alcoholic say that the only thing he needs to do is to keep sober. Certainly he <u>must</u> keep sober, for there will be no home if he doesn't. But he is yet a long way from making good to the wife or

parents whom for years he has so shockingly treated. (82)

19. Yes, there is a long period of reconstruction ahead. We must take the lead. A remorseful mumbling that we are sorry won't fill the bill at all. We ought to sit down with the family and frankly analyze the past as we now see it, being very careful not to criticize them. Their defects may be glaring, but the chances are that our own actions are partly responsible. So we clean house with the family, asking each morning in meditation that our Creator show us the way of patience, tolerance, kindliness and love. (83)

20. The spiritual life is not a theory. **WE HAVE TO LIVE IT.** Unless one's family expresses a desire to live upon spiritual principles we think we ought not to urge them. We should not talk incessantly to them about spiritual matters. They will change in time. Our behavior will convince them more than our words. We must remember that ten or twenty years of drunkenness would make a skeptic out of anyone. (83)

21. It is easy to let up on the spiritual program of action and rest on our laurels. We are headed for trouble if we do, for alcohol is a subtle foe. We are not cured of alcoholism. What we really have is a daily reprieve contingent on the maintenance of our spiritual condition. Every day is a day when we must carry the vision of God's will into all of our activities. *"How can I best serve Thee--Thy will (not mine) be done."* These are thoughts which must go with us constantly. We can exercise our will power along this line all we wish. It is

the proper use of the will. (85)

22. Much has already been said about receiving strength, inspiration, and direction from Him who has all knowledge and power. If we have carefully followed directions, we have begun to sense the flow of His Spirit into us. To some extent we have become God-conscious. We have begun to develop this vital sixth sense. But we _must_ go further and that means more action. (85)

23. When we retire at night, we constructively review our day. Were we resentful, selfish, dishonest or afraid? Do we owe an apology? Have we kept something to ourselves which should be discussed with another person at once? Were we kind and loving toward all? What could we have done better? Were we thinking of ourselves most of the time? Or were we thinking of what we could do for others, of what we could pack into the stream of life? But we _must_ be careful not to drift into worry, remorse or morbid reflection, for that would diminish our usefulness to others . After making our review we ask God's forgiveness and inquire what corrective measures should be taken. (86)

24. Life will take on new meaning. To watch people recover, to see them help others, to watch loneliness vanish, to see a fellowship grow up about you, to have a host of friends-this is an experience you _must_ not miss. We know you will not want to miss it. Frequent contact with newcomers and with each other is the bright spot of our lives. (89)

25. To be vital, faith <u>must</u> be accompanied by self sacrifice and unselfish, constructive action. (93)

26. These things will come to pass naturally and in good time provided, however, the alcoholic continues to demonstrate that he can be sober, considerate, and helpful, regardless of what anyone says or does. Of course, we all fall much below this standard many times. But we <u>must</u> try to repair the damage immediately lest we pay the penalty by a spree. (99)

27. If there be divorce or separation, there should be no undue haste for the couple to get together. The man should be sure of his recovery. The wife should fully understand his new way of life. If their old relationship is to be resumed it <u>must</u> be on a better basis, since the former did not work. This means a new attitude and spirit all around. (99)

28. Both you and the new man <u>must</u> walk day by day in the path of spiritual progress. (100)

29. Wait until repeated stumbling convinces him he <u>must</u> act, for the more you hurry him the longer his recovery may be delayed. (113)

30. Though it is infinitely better that he have no relapse at all, as has been true with many of our men, it is by no means a bad thing in some cases. Your husband will see at once that he <u>must</u> redouble his spiritual activities if he expects to survive. (120)

31. The head of the house ought to remember that he is mainly to blame for what befell his home. He can scarcely square the account in his lifetime. But he <u>must</u> see the danger of over-concentration on financial success. Although financial recovery is on the way for many of us, we found we could not place money first. For us, material well-being always followed spiritual progress; it never preceded. (127)

32. Since the home has suffered more than anything else , it is well that a man exert himself there. He is not likely to get far in any direction if he fails to show unselfishness and love under his own roof. We know there are difficult wives and families, but the man who is getting over alcoholism <u>must</u> remember *he did much to make them so.* (127)

33. We have come to believe He would like us to keep our heads in the clouds with Him, but that our feet ought to be firmly planted on earth. That is where our fellow travelers are, and that is where our work <u>must</u> be done. (130)

34. If your man accepts your offer, it should be pointed out that physical treatment is but a small part of the picture. Though you are providing him with the best possible medical attention, he should understand that he <u>must</u> undergo a change of heart. To get over drinking will require a transformation of thought and attitude. **We all had to place recovery above everything**, for without recovery we would have lost both home and business. (143)

35. When the man is presented with this volume it is best that no one tell him he <u>must</u> abide by its suggestions. The man must decide for himself. (144)

36. Long experience with alcoholic excuses naturally arouses suspicion. When his wife next calls saying he is sick, you may jump to the conclusion he is drunk. If he is, and is still trying to recover, he will tell you about it even if it means the loss of his job. For he knows he <u>must</u> be honest if he would live at all. (146)

37. We have shown how we got out from under. You say, "Yes, I'm willing. But am I to be consigned to a life where I shall be stupid, boring and glum, like some righteous people I see? I know I <u>must</u> get along without liquor, but how can I? Have you a sufficient substitute?" (152)

38. But life was not easy for the two friends. Plenty of difficulties presented themselves. Both saw that they <u>must</u> keep spiritually active. One day they called up the head nurse of a local hospital. They explained their need and inquired if she had a first class alcoholic prospect. (156)

39. Though they knew they <u>must</u> help other alcoholics if they would remain sober, that motive became secondary. It was transcended by the happiness they found in giving themselves for others. (159)

40. Still you may say: "But I will not have the benefit of contact with you who wrote this book." We cannot

be sure. God will determine that, so you <u>must</u> remember that your real reliance is always upon Him. He will show you how to create the fellowship you crave. (164)

"Still you may say: "But I will not have the benefit of contact with you who write this book." We cannot be sure. God will determine that, so you <u>must</u> remember that your real reliance is always upon Him. He will show you how to create the fellowship you crave.

Our book is meant to be suggestive only. We realize we know only a little. God will constantly disclose more to you and to us. Ask Him in your morning meditation what you can do each day for the man who is still sick. The answers will come, if your own house is in order. But obviously you cannot transmit something you haven't got.

See to it that your relationship with Him is right, and great events will come to pass for you and countless others. This is the Great Fact for us. Abandon yourself to God as you understand God. Admit your faults to Him and to your fellows. Clear away the wreckage of your past.

Give freely of what you find and join us. We shall be with you in the **Fellowship of the Spirit**, and you will surely meet some of us as you trudge the Road of Happy Destiny. May God bless you and keep you - until then."
~Big Book Pg. 164

The Serenity Prayer

God grant me the serenity

To accept the things I cannot change;

Courage to change the things I can;

And wisdom to know the difference.

Living one day at a time;

Enjoying one moment at a time;

Accepting hardships as the pathway to peace;

Taking, as He did,

this sinful world As it is,

not as I would have it;

Trusting that He will make all things right

If I surrender to His Will;

So that I may be reasonably happy in this life

And supremely happy with Him

Forever and ever in the next.

Amen.

(prayer attributed to Reinhold Neibuhr, 1892-1971)

Made in the USA
Columbia, SC
19 October 2020

23115153R00045